MEN COLORING BOOK

COLORING BOOK GIFT FOR MEN, DADS, FATHERS, HUSBANDS AND SPECIAL MEN EVERYWHERE

BELLA MOSLEY

D1317158

ISBN-13: 978-1519145369

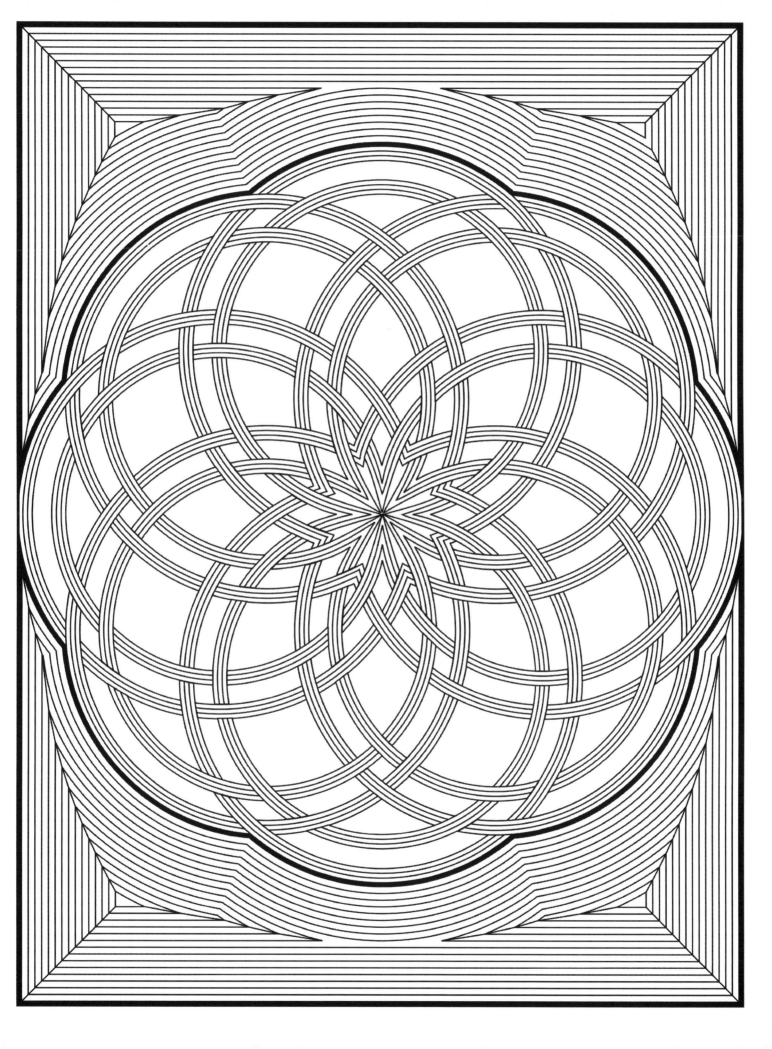

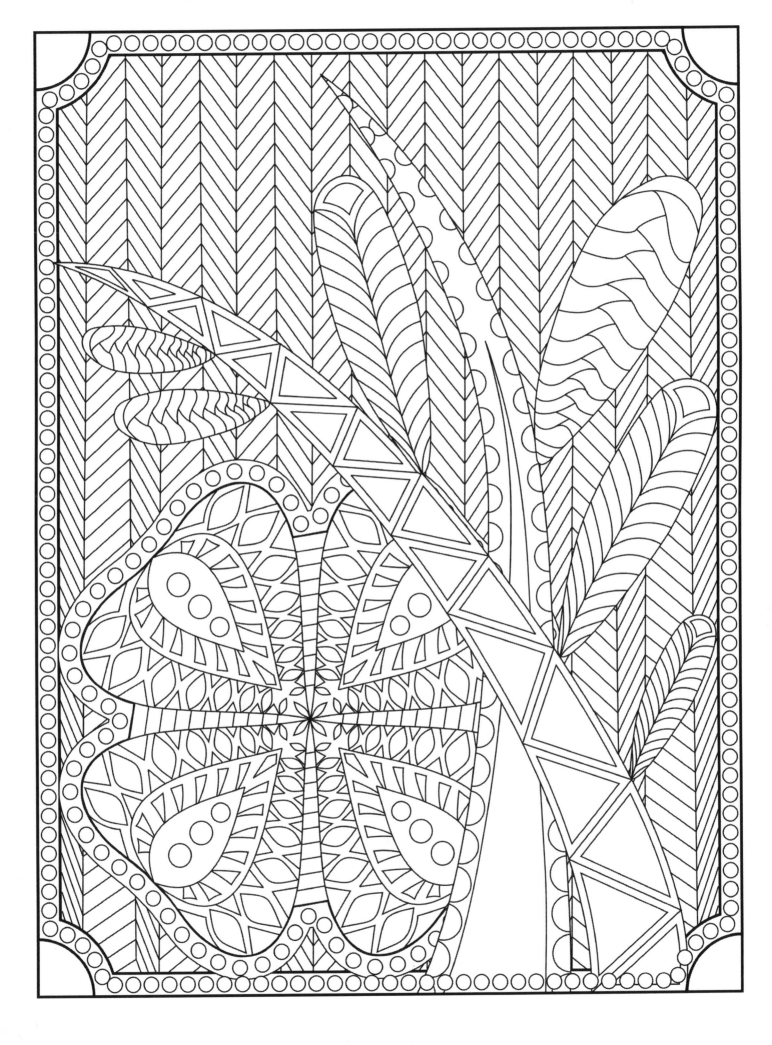

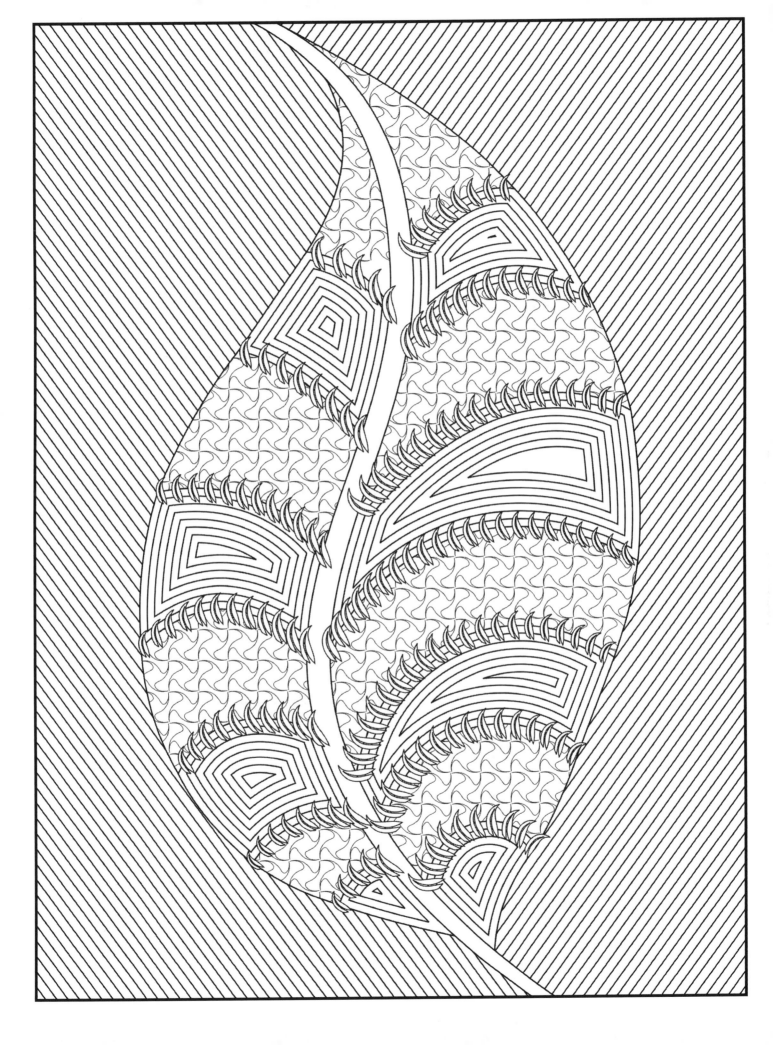

COLORING TIPS

1. Find a quiet place to do your coloring.

2. Choose your colors according to your liking. Be light and open-minded.

3. Choose to color in bright natural light whenever possible.

4. Make sure you are sitting in a comfortable seat with good back support. Relax.

5. Don't be afraid to express your creativity. Stress relief coloring is all about fun.

6. Pick your favorite pattern to color.

7. Color at a time when you are less likely to be interrupted.

8. If you like classical music, switch it on and play it softly in the background.

9. Choose coloring pencils over regular crayons to do your coloring

10. If you like to use art markers, it is best to use a sheet of craft plastic under the coloring page.

11. Stop coloring whenever you feel like stopping.

12. Whatever the outcomes, it is your masterpiece. Cut it out and frame it if you so desire.

NOTE:

In order to prevent color-bleeding no images were placed on the opposite side of each artwork.

THANK YOU!

Made in the USA
Middletown, DE
22 December 2015